PRESOV

City Delight Travel Guide (2023)

"Unveiling the Charms of Slovakia's Historic Gem – Your Essential Presov Adventure"

BY:

Ralph I. Dowell

The Presov City Delight Travel Guide is pleased to welcome you in 2023. Discover the hidden treasures, vibrant culture, and stunning scenery of this alluring Slovakian location as we take you on a voyage of discovery.

With its inspiration, you may explore Presov City's bustling festivals and ancient streets, making your trip a memorable excursion.

Copyright © 2023

ISBN: **9798857603178**

Contents

Introduction

Welcome to Presov City, a little-known treasure tucked away in Slovakia's east. Presov, which is steeped in history and surrounded by breathtaking natural scenery, provides visitors looking for a balance of culture, adventure, and calm with a distinctive and genuine experience.

With the help of this thorough travel guide, you can discover the city's hidden gems, maximize your time there, and form lifelong memories.

Greetings from Presov City

Presov City's quaint appeal and kind welcome will capture your attention as soon as you arrive. The third-largest city in Slovakia, Presov, has a long and illustrious history that began in the thirteenth century. The name of the city is derived from the Slovak word "pre," which means "burnt," in honor of its historical function as a fortified village that guarded the area from invaders.

A fascinating fusion of the past and contemporary may be found at Presov. Visitors will have a pleasant and delightful stay thanks to the vivid contemporary amenities and the well-preserved historic center's cobblestone walkways and vibrant façade. The city is a mesmerizing destination for culture fans due to the distinctive fusion of Slovak, Ruthenian, and

Hungarian influences that can be sensed in its customs, architecture, and food.

Concerning Slovakia

Landlocked Slovakia, sometimes referred to as the Slovak Republic, is a nation in Central Europe. Slovakia has a varied geography that includes the magnificent Carpathian Mountains as well as lush plains and attractive valleys. Slovakia is bordered by Poland to the north, Ukraine to the east, Hungary to the south, Austria to the southwest, and the Czech Republic to the west.

Before obtaining independence in 1993, the nation has a long and colorful history, having been a part of the Great Moravian Empire, the Austro-Hungarian Empire, and Czechoslovakia. Slovakia is well known for its picturesque villages, UNESCO-listed wooden churches, and medieval castles that offer an insight into its historical history.

The folklore, music, dance, and traditional crafts that make up Slovakia's culture are all commemorated annually via a variety of festivals and events. Slovakia is a lovely nation to tour and get to know the locals in because of its kind, welcoming, and patriotic population.

Why Travel to Presov City?

Presov City is a captivating location that appeals to a variety of interests, making it a great option for tourists looking for a varied experience. Visit Presov for these compelling causes:

Rich History: Presov has a history that spans eight centuries, and much of its medieval beauty has been preserved. Explore the ruins of the old city walls, marvel at the church architecture, and meander through the historic center's winding lanes to get a sense of the city's past.

Presov provides a wonderful fusion of customs, food, and languages as a melting pot of the Slovak, Ruthenian, and Hungarian civilizations. Witness the peaceful cohabitation of several ethnic groups and the distinctive cultural treasures they provide to the city.

Nature and adventure: Presov City, which is surrounded by beautiful landscapes, becomes a great starting point for exploring the neighboring natural treasures. Outdoor enthusiasts will find a variety of activities to partake in, from hiking in the High Tatras to skiing in the winter.

Events & Festivals: Throughout the year, Presov holds a number of festivals and cultural gatherings that include local crafts, cuisine, music, and dancing. Experience the best of the local culture by taking part in these vibrant festivals.

Warmth & Hospitality: The residents of Presov are well known for their warmth and friendliness. Interact with the populace, discover their traditions, and take in the welcoming ambiance that permeates the city.

This travel guide offers comprehensive details about Presov City's attractions, lodging alternatives, food options, and useful advice for a comfortable and pleasurable trip.

It is intended to help you get the most out of your trip. Presov City guarantees a memorable experience that will leave a deep impact on your heart, whether you are a history enthusiast, a nature lover, or a cultural traveler.

Chapter 1

Organizing Your Travel

The Best Time to Go

It's crucial to pick the ideal time of year to visit Presov City if you want to maximize your vacation enjoyment. The best time to book your vacation will depend significantly on the city's temperature and seasonal attractions.

Spring (March to May): Spring is a beautiful time of year to visit Presov City since the weather starts to warm up and the landscapes start to bloom with vibrant colors. With a comfortable temperature range of 10°C to 20°C (50°F to 68°F), it's the ideal time to engage in outdoor sports and see the city's historical attractions.

Summer (June to August): In Presov, summer is the busiest travel period. Temperatures range from 20°C to 30°C (68°F to 86°F), making it a warm day. The greatest time to go trekking, go on outdoor excursions, and go to many cultural festivals and events in and around the city is now.

Autumn (September to November): Fall is still a fantastic season to explore Presov City. The skies are still clear, and the surroundings are painted in a stunning tapestry of autumnal hues. Starting to drop are the temperatures, which are between

10°C and 20°C (50°F and 68°F). It's a terrific time to get outside and take part in fall activities.

Winter (December to February): Presov experiences a chilly, snowy winter with temperatures between -5°C and 5°C (23°F and 41°F). This is the perfect time to travel if you prefer winter sports like skiing and snowboarding because the neighboring High Tatras provide fantastic skiing chances.

Transportation to Presov City

By Air

There is no airport in Presov City. However, Kosice International Airport (KSC), which is situated about 36 kilometers (22 miles) southwest of Presov, is the closest international airport. Kosice is the most practical entry point into the region since a number of airlines offer frequent domestic and international flights to and from there. *It is possible to go to Presov City from Kosice International Airport by:*

Taxi: Depending on traffic, a taxi ride to Presov will take between 30 and 40 minutes from the airport.

Bus: The airport is connected to Presov via frequent bus services. Tickets may be bought at the airport or on the bus, and the trip lasts about an hour.

Via Train

Train connections to several places in Slovakia and its surrounding countries are excellent from Presov City. Presov Railway Station, the city's primary train station, is situated in the city's center, making it simple to go to the city's attractions from there.

Trains inside Slovakia: Bratislava, Kosice, and Poprad are just a few of the important cities that are regularly served by Slovak Railways (ZSSK)'s domestic rail service.

International Trains: From nearby cities like Budapest (Hungary), Krakow (Poland), and

Vienna (Austria), there are direct train connections.

By Bus:

An extensive bus network connects Presov City to several cities and villages in Slovakia and its surrounding countries on a regular basis.

Domestic Buses: Presov Bus Station, the primary bus hub, is close to the city center and provides frequent connections to other significant Slovak cities.

International Buses: Presov is connected to a number of countries by international buses, including Hungary, Poland, the Czech Republic, and Austria.

Navigating Presov City

Presov City is conveniently small and accessible by foot. Most of the major sites and the city's core are accessible by foot. Furthermore, Presov boasts a trustworthy public transit network that includes buses and trolleybuses, making it simple to go throughout the city.

Public transit: The city has an effective and reasonably priced public transit system. Onboard the buses and trolleybuses, ticket machines at stops are available for ticket purchases.

Taxi: Taxis may be hailed on the street or reserved through taxi companies, and they are also accessible around the city. To ensure a fair fare, it is advised to utilize authorized taxis equipped with meters.

Car Rental: Presov City is home to a number of car rental agencies if you prefer the independence of driving yourself. However, be aware that parking may not always be abundant.

Visa necessities and advice for traveling

Visa prerequisites

Travelers from numerous nations do not require a visa for brief visits *(up to 90 days)* for tourism as Slovakia is a member of the Schengen Area. Prior to going, it is important to confirm the precise visa requirements for your country of citizenship.

Verify that your passport is still valid at least six months after the day you want to exit Slovakia.

Travel Advice

Even though many people in tourist destinations understand English, learning a few basic Slovak words will improve your relationships with locals and demonstrate your respect for their culture.

The Euro (EUR) is the official currency of Slovakia. Although most businesses take credit cards, it's usually a good idea to have extra cash on hand, particularly in smaller towns or when buying from local sellers.

Respect Local Customs: Due to Slovakia's rich cultural legacy, it is important to observe and uphold regional traditions and customs. When visiting holy locations, dress modestly, and never photograph someone without their consent.

Health and Safety: The healthcare system in Slovakia is dependable. It is advised to have travel insurance that includes medical emergencies. Although bottled water is widely accessible and typically safe to consume, tap water is also an option.

Consider the weather when packing, depending on the season you travel. Bring lightweight clothing, sunscreen, and a hat for the summer, while the winter calls for thick layers, a quality coat, and winter accessories.

Save the local emergency numbers for the police, the ambulance service, and the embassy or consulate of your nation in Slovakia in case of an emergency.

You may maximize your time in Presov City by organizing your vacation well in advance and being well-prepared. This will help you develop priceless experiences that will last a lifetime. Travel safely!

Chapter 2

Options for lodging

Presov City has a wide variety of lodging choices to fit any traveler's needs and price range. The city has plenty to offer, whether you're looking for opulent comfort, homey charm, or something genuinely special. The many lodging choices in Presov are as follows:

Expensive Inns and Resorts

Presov offers a variety of stylish luxury hotels and resorts that cater to guests who like indulgence and pampering and offer first-rate facilities and individualized services. These homes frequently have excellent locations with breathtaking views and easy access to the city's attractions.

Features of upscale resorts and hotels:

Large, well-designed rooms with contemporary comforts including flat-screen TVs, comfortable mattresses, and opulent bathrooms. onsite dining establishments serving great wines and gourmet food. Spa and wellness centers for relaxation and rejuvenation with a variety of treatments, saunas, and workout facilities. other leisure amenities, including pools. Concierge services to help with reservations for restaurants, transportation, and tours.

Mid-Range Inns and B&Bs

For tourists looking for cozy, cheap lodging without sacrificing quality, mid-range hotels and guesthouses are a popular option. These establishments provide a comfortable stay and are frequently owned by families, creating a cozy and inviting ambiance.

Mid-Range Hotel and Guesthouse Amenities: comfortable accommodations with satellite TV, Wi-Fi, and private bathrooms. Breakfast is included in the accommodation charge and frequently includes both international and regional selections. On-site restaurants featuring regional and foreign cuisine may be available at some midrange hotels. Staff that is informed and helpful and may offer advice on the area. Cozy common spaces for guests to unwind and mingle with other tourists.

Accommodations That Are Affordable

With a selection of hostels and low-cost motels, Presov City also accommodates guests on a tight budget. Backpackers, lone travelers, or those who like to spend less on lodging so they have more money to explore the city would love these possibilities.

Characteristics of
Affordable Accommodations

individual rooms with shared facilities or dorm-style rooms.

There are common amenities for visitors to use, including kitchens, lounges, and restrooms. Some low-cost hotels could provide a basic breakfast or have a cafe on site that serves inexpensive food. Ideal for meeting new people and sharing travel experiences. Excellent option for tourists who want to spend the most of their time sightseeing and require a cozy location to sleep at night.

Original and Fun Accommodations

Presov has some unorthodox and eccentric lodging alternatives that guarantee to make your stay unforgettable if you want a really unique and memorable experience.

Features of Distinctive and Fun Hotels

Historical structures that have been restored, such as castles, mansions, or country cottages, provide a window into the area's past. eco-friendly lodgings, including eco-lodges or sustainable guesthouses, where visitors may learn about ethical tourism. Glamping locations, which combine luxurious accommodations with camping, let you spend the night close to nature without sacrificing comfort.

Strangely themed lodgings with a sense of adventure and surprise, such treehouses, yurts, or warm cottages.

Farm stays provide visitors the chance to experience rural life firsthand, get involved in farming, and eat locally produced food. Regardless of the kind of lodging you select in Presov City, make sure to reserve in advance, especially during the busiest travel times, to obtain the greatest selections. Keep in mind that the sort of lodging you choose will greatly affect your whole trip experience, so while making your decision, take your tastes, budget, and desired degree of comfort into account. Create enduring recollections throughout your time in Presov City and take pleasure in this alluring location!

Chapter 3

Investigating Presov City

Presov City is a fascinating tourist destination since it offers a lovely combination of historical sites, cultural attractions, scenic beauty, and gastronomic pleasures. The following are a few must-see locations and activities that will enhance your tour of Presov:

Preslav Historical Center

The old district of Presov is a veritable architectural treasure trove, with endearing squares and cobblestone lanes that transport you to another era. Walk through the cobblestone lanes, take in the beautifully maintained structures, and become lost in the history of the area.

Hlavna Street

The primary thoroughfare and bustling center of activity in Presov's historic district is Hlavna Street. It is the ideal area to engage in some people-watching, sample local cuisine, and pick up souvenirs because it is lined with vibrant facades, stores, cafés, and restaurants.

The Cathedral of St. Nicholas

The St. Nicholas Cathedral, a marvel of Gothic design, dominates the city's skyline. The lavish interior of this building, which is decorated with elaborate murals, sculptures, and a beautiful altar, complements its remarkable façade. Views of the entire city may be had by ascending the bell tower.

Wine Cellar Road

Visits to Presov's Wine Cellar Road are essential for wine lovers. This charming path goes to historic wine cellars outside the city where you can sample regional wines, learn about winemaking, and take in the lovely landscape.

Presov's Museums and Galleries, section

Presov is home to a number of galleries and museums that help visitors understand the city's history, culture, and creative legacy better.

Museum of Ruthenian Culture at the Slovak National Museum

This museum, which is situated in the historic district, highlights the distinctive Ruthenian culture of the area. Learn about the traditions and rituals of the nearby Ruthenian people while exploring traditional clothing, folk art, and religious objects.

Museum of Miklus Prison

Take a trip down memory lane and learn about the gruesome past of Miklus Prison, which housed political prisoners during World War II. The museum offers information on the repressive government of the era as well as the experiences of people who endured suffering there.

Green Spaces and Parks

With its parks and green areas, Presov provides a welcome respite from the city, allowing you to unwind, take in the scenery, and appreciate the city's natural beauty.

Trbské Pleso Park, section

Trbské Pleso Park is a tranquil oasis with walking pathways, a lake, and seats where you can relax and take in the scenery close to the city center.

Alpinka Park

Family-friendly amenities including playgrounds, sports courts, and attractive gardens can be found at Alpinka Park. It's the perfect location for a stroll or a picnic.

Places of Worship

Numerous religious locations can be found in Presov City, which reflects the city's eclectic background.

The Greek Catholic Church of St. John the Baptist

This magnificent wooden church, which is also a UNESCO World Heritage site, is a spectacular example of Eastern Orthodox architecture. Explore the church's interior and take in the exquisite woodwork carvings and religious symbolism.

Presov Orthodox Synagogue

The synagogue, a reminder of the once-vibrant Jewish community in the city, today serves as a hub for culture and education. Discover the intriguing design and history of this structure, which demonstrates the wide range of religious traditions in Presov.

Presov's Regional Food & Dining

Traditional recipes and strong tastes combine to create the delicious Slovak food. Presov City has a variety of dining establishments to suit your preferences.

Classic Slovak
Dining Establishments

Enjoy traditional Slovak cuisine, like Bryndzové Haluky (potato dumplings with sheep cheese), Kapustnica (cabbage soup with sausages), and a variety of meat dishes. Local beers and wines are frequently served as a complement to the cuisine.

Cuisine from Around the World

Additionally, Presov provides a wide variety of different cuisines, such as Italian, Mexican, Asian, and more. Discover the different eateries and cafés dotted across the city for a taste of the world's cuisine.

Presov City's shopping

Presov offers a variety of shopping options, whether you're seeking for contemporary retail therapy or traditional handicrafts.

Neighborhood markets and gift shops

To find homemade crafts, fresh vegetables, and artisanal goods, visit local markets. Don't forget to get some customary trinkets like wooden toys, pottery from Slovakia, and embroidered goods.

Contemporary Malls

Visit one of the city's shopping centers for a more up-to-date shopping experience. There, you can discover well-known retailers, apparel boutiques, and electronics stores.

You will certainly be fascinated by Presov City's rich history, varied cultural offers, and friendly people after exploring it. Spend some time enjoying each encounter and soaking in the distinctive character of this alluring Slovakian city.

Chapter 4

Prerov City day trips

Presov City is a great starting point from which to explore the neighboring areas, each of which has its own distinctive attractions and experiences. From Presov, you can take the following fascinating day trips:

Five. Bardejov

A UNESCO World Heritage site, Bardejov is a picturesque medieval village 35 kilometers *(22 miles)* northwest of Presov known for its maintained historical architecture and cultural value.

Town Square in Bardejov

Radnicne namestie, Bardejov's breathtaking Town Square, is the city's center. It has the old Town Hall, fine Renaissance and Gothic homes, and the well-known Gothic Basilica of St. Giles, all of which are surrounded by colorful structures. Enjoy the scenery while strolling casually across the area and consider relaxing at one of the cafés that line the square.

Wooden Churches on the UNESCO List

There are a number of UNESCO-listed wooden churches in the Carpathian area close to Bardejov. These distinctive churches are works of religious art and timber building. Don't forget to see the St. Egidius Church in Lukov, the St. Michael

Church in Ladomirová, and the St. Francis of Assisi Church in Hervartov.

High Tatras National Park

A day excursion to the High Tatras National Park is essential for outdoor enthusiasts. The park, which is located around 65 kilometers (40 miles) northwest of Presov, has stunning scenery and a wide range of outdoor activities.

Nature Trails and Hiking Routes

With a network of clearly indicated routes that are suitable for walkers of all fitness levels and experience levels, the High Tatras is a hiker and nature enthusiast's dream come true. The park offers activities for all levels of fitness, including strenuous peak climbs as well as leisurely stroll around alpine lakes.

Winter sports and skiing

The High Tatras become a beautiful paradise throughout the winter months. Tatranská Lomnica and Trbské Pleso are two ski resorts that provide fantastic skiing and snowboarding options. In the magnificent snowy landscapes, you may also attempt snowshoeing, sledding, and snowmobiling.

Levoca

Levoca, another picturesque medieval town that enchants visitors with its rich history and well-preserved architecture, is located about 36 kilometers (22 miles) southwest of Presov.

St. James Church

The magnificent St. James Church is Levoca's main attraction. The largest wooden Gothic altar in the entire world, expertly crafted by Master Paul of Levoca, may be found in this gothic cathedral. Additionally, the church tower's 360-degree views of the city and its surroundings are available.

Levoca Town Walls

Investigate the 13th-century town walls, which have been intact. Enjoy the picturesque views of the town's roofs and the surrounding greenery as you stroll around the fortifications.

Kosice

Slovak Republic's second-largest city, Kosice, is situated around 70 kilometers (43 miles) to the southeast of Presov. It is a bustling metropolis with a varied cultural background and a long history.

Saint Elisabeth Cathedral

The St. Elisabeth Cathedral is a magnificent work of architecture and is the biggest Gothic cathedral in Slovakia. Atop the cathedral tower, you may get a bird's-eye perspective of Kosice and the surrounding area.

Singing Fountain

The Singing Fountain is a well-liked tourist destination that presents breathtaking water, light, and music performances. It is situated in the center of Kosice. It's a wonderful place to unwind and take in the breathtaking nighttime shows.

Presov City day tours provide a wide variety of activities, from getting lost in history to discovering stunning natural settings. Each location has its own distinct attraction and charm, ensuring a fascinating and enlightening experience. Take use of your stay in Presov by discovering the treasures outside of its boundaries.

Chapter 5

Outdoor & Adventure Activities

Both nature lovers and adrenaline seekers can find plenty of thrilling outdoor activities in Presov City and the surrounding area. Embrace the breathtaking scenery and heart-pounding sensations with these wonderful activities:

Routes for Hiking and Trekking

With its gorgeous surroundings and vast network of clearly designated routes that accommodate hikers and trekkers of all skill levels, the area surrounding Presov is a hiker and trekker's dream. Set off on fascinating travels over the Carpathian Mountains and beyond by lacing up your hiking boots.

Several well-traveled hiking and trekking trails are

The High Tatras are traversed by the famous Tatranska Magistrala, which provides breath-taking vistas of the towering peaks, glacial lakes, and verdant valleys. It might take many days to finish the difficult trek.

Slovak Paradise National Park offers an exhilarating hiking experience and is renowned for its craggy gorges, waterfalls, and wooden ladders. The Sucha Bela Gorge and the Hornad Canyon shouldn't be missed.

Pieniny National Park: Take a stroll down the Dunajec River Gorge to take in this area's breathtaking splendor. The walk provides breathtaking views of the river running through the valley and the limestone cliffs.

Mountain biking and cycling

Cycling aficionados may choose from a variety of gorgeous routes, from easy rural drives to strenuous mountain bike tracks.

Bike Routes Around Presov: Discover the surrounding area by riding over a number of routes that pass through quaint towns, sweeping farmland, and verdant meadows.

Cycling in the High Tatras: For lovers of mountain riding, the High Tatras provide exhilarating tracks with varied topography and sweeping views of the surrounding peaks.

Hornad River White Water Rafting

Consider white water rafting on Slovakia's Hornad River, one of its longest rivers, if you're looking for some aquatic action. Enjoy the rush of sailing over waterfalls and rapids while surrounded by breathtaking natural beauty.

Experienced guides that ensure your safety while offering an amazing experience plan white water rafting trips. It's the perfect activity for teams, families, and individuals seeking for a burst of excitement and a chance to get outside and enjoy nature.

Winter Activities in the Nearby Mountains

Winter sports aficionados use the nearby mountains as a playground throughout the winter. A variety of activities are available to enjoy the wintry paradise in the High Tatras and the adjacent ski resorts.

Take to the slopes in well-known ski resorts like Trbské Pleso, Tatranská Lomnica, and Vysoke Tatry. Skiing and snowboarding. These resorts provide a variety of lines and terrain to accommodate skiers and snowboarders of all abilities.

Cross-Country Skiing: Enjoy the peace and quiet of cross-country skiing on groomed paths in the High Tatras or other picturesque areas around Presov.

Snowshoeing: Wander through snow-covered mountains and woods while you take in the beauty of winter sceneries.

Ice Climbing: The frozen waterfalls in the High Tatras offer experienced climbers a difficult and rewarding ice climbing experience.

In and around Presov City, adventure and outdoor pursuits offer wonderful chances to come in touch with nature, push yourself, and make priceless memories. Presov's breathtaking surroundings have plenty to offer everyone, whether you're an experienced outdoor enthusiast or a beginner looking for new adventures. Enjoy the pleasure of exploring this alluring area, but don't forget to verify local laws and safety precautions.

Chapter 6

Cultural Festivals and Events

Presov City and the area around it come alive with lively cultural celebrations that honor the customs, music, arts, and regional history. By participating in these celebrations, you have the exceptional chance to get fully immersed in the region's rich cultural heritage and make priceless memories. The following are some of the major festivals and cultural events that are held in and around Presov:

Seventh Presov Folklore Festival

An annual celebration of traditional folk music, dancing, and crafts is held at the Presov Folklore Festival. The event, which usually takes place in June or July throughout the summer, draws visitors from all around Slovakia and its surrounding nations. The city center serves as the event's primary location, where lively performances by folk ensembles, dance companies, and musicians take place on outdoor stages.

The event brings lively parades, traditional costumes, and exhibitions highlighting folk art, crafts, and regional specialties to Presov. A broad range of folk customs are on display for visitors to see, including Slovak dances and melodies as well as ethnic dances from Ruthenian, Ukrainian, and Hungarian populations. The Presov Folklore Festival offers a real-world look into the rich cultural variety of Slovakia.

Pohoda Music Festival

One of Slovakia's biggest and most well-known music events, the Pohoda Music Festival draws music lovers from all around Europe. Annually, it takes place in July at the Trenn Airport, which is located 93 miles (150 kilometers) west of Presov. The word "pohoda," which translates to "well-being" in Slovak, represents the festival's laid-back and welcoming environment.

The Pohoda Music Festival has a diverse roster of both local and international performers from a variety of musical genres, including jazz, world music, rock, pop, and electronic. The festival offers theatrical plays, seminars, conversations on social and environmental concerns, and music performances in addition to those.

People of various ages and backgrounds are drawn to Pohoda because of its lively and welcoming atmosphere, which makes it a great cultural event. The festival's distinctive fusion of music, art, and social interaction gives visitors an outstanding experience.

Wine-related events and festivals

Numerous wine festivals and celebrations are held all year long throughout Slovakia's wine-producing areas, including the Presov region, particularly during the grape-harvesting season.

Visitors may sample a broad range of wines, from crisp whites to strong reds, as local winemakers display their best offerings. Wine lovers and culture seekers will both enjoy the joyful environment that is enhanced by traditional folk music, dancing, and cuisine.

The "Vinum Galiciae" festival, which takes place in Medzilaborce, some 50 kilometers (31 miles) northeast of Presov, is one of the prominent wine celebrations. Wine tastings, cultural events, and delectable fare are all part of the festival, which honors the wines of the Zemplin wine area.

These cultural gatherings and festivals offer a fascinating window into Slovakia's rich and varied cultural history and its people. By taking part in the festivities, you'll not only have a memorable time but also have a greater understanding of the customs and inventiveness that make this area so special.

Chapter 7

Nightlife and entertainment in Presov

Presov City has a vibrant and varied nightlife scene that appeals to both residents and tourists. Presov has something for everyone, whether you're searching for a quiet evening at a welcoming bar, a night of dancing and music at a nightclub, or a cultural performance at the theater. The following are some of the city's top nightlife and entertainment options:

Pubs and Bars

The taverns and pubs in Presov offer a friendly and welcoming environment for mingling, having a drink, and taking in the local culture. Since many of these businesses are situated in and around the historical core, both locals and visitors may readily reach them.

In Presov, some well-liked taverns and pubs are as follows

Irish bar U Zeleného stromu: This real Irish bar serves up a variety of beers, alcoholic beverages, and traditional Irish food. It is a favorite hangout for both residents and visitors because to live music performances, helpful staff, and a pleasant atmosphere.

Sky Bar Presov: Located on the roof of a structure in the heart of the city, Sky Bar offers breathtaking views of the surroundings. Drink a selection of drinks, beers, and wines while admiring the beautiful surroundings.

Zmerta tavern: This unconventional and one-of-a-kind tavern has a lively and laid-back environment thanks to its odd artwork and antique memorabilia decor. Live music performances, poetry readings, and open mic nights are frequently held at Zmerta Pub.

Restauracia u Holubov: This quaint eatery and tavern, housed in a historic structure, offers a variety of beers and traditional Slovak fare. It's a well-liked location for both daytime and evening visitors because to the warm interior and outside seats.

Clubs & Dance Locations

Presov offers a variety of nightclubs and dance locations for people looking for a night of dancing and exciting entertainment. These locations come alive with music, DJs, and excited people, giving partygoers an exhilarating experience.

The lively nightclub Club DUNA, which is in the heart of the city, offers themed events, DJ performances, and live music. It accommodates a variety of likes and preferences with various dance floors and a variety of musical styles.

Ná Club: Another well-liked nightlife spot, Ná Club is renowned for its upbeat vibe and danceable music. Special occasions, themed parties, and live concerts by regional and worldwide performers are frequently held there.

As its name indicates, Retro Club Presov transports patrons back in time to the greatest tunes of the 1980s and 1990s. It's a terrific location for people who appreciate listening to vintage music and dancing to it.

Theaters and cultural performances make up

Presov is home to a number of cultural centers and theaters that provide a variety of activities, including plays, concerts, and art exhibits. These places are ideal for anyone who wants to enjoy the arts and become immersed in the community's cultural life.

The Joná Záborsk Theatre presents a range of productions, including musicals, comedies, dances, and dramas. Take in top-notch performances by regional and national performers in a lovely, private environment.

PKO - Park Kultry an Odychu: PKO is a cultural hub that hosts a variety of cultural events throughout the year, including performances, festivals, exhibits, and more. To learn about forthcoming shows and other entertainment alternatives, consult their schedule.

Visit Cinemax Presov, a cutting-edge movie theater complex that shows the newest Hollywood blockbusters and foreign films, if you're a movie buff.

The nightlife and entertainment scene in Presov provides a fantastic fusion of modern experiences and classic cultural treats. Presov provides everything you need for a pleasurable and unforgettable night out, whether you choose to unwind with friends at a bar, dance the night away at a nightclub, or immerse yourself in the arts and cultural acts.

Useful Information

Knowing the vital facts that will guarantee a simple and pleasurable journey is crucial when visiting Presov City in Slovakia. The following are some critical details to bear in mind:

Emergency Phone Numbers:

It's essential to have the local emergency contacts on hand in Presov in case of any emergencies:

112 Police

111 ambulance

112 Fire Department

The emergency number in Slovakia is 112, which links you to all emergency services in Europe. The majority of operators are fluent in English and other foreign languages.

Healthcare Facilities and Drugstores

To meet the demands of travelers' health, Presov City has pharmacies and medical centers with the necessary equipment:

Nemocnicna 1, 080 01 Presov is the address of the Presov Hospital (Nemocnica sv. Alzbety Presov).
Tel: +421 51 772 6111

In general, pharmacies are open during regular business hours and are dispersed around the city (Lekaren). On a rotating basis, some bigger pharmacies could provide 24-hour service. To find them, look for the green cross symbol.

Having comprehensive travel insurance that includes medical evacuation and repatriation is advised. Regarding precise coverage details and contact information for emergencies, check with your insurance company.

Regional Traditions and Etiquette

In order to respect local customs and etiquette while visiting Presov City in Slovakia, one must be aware of the following:

When introducing yourself, shake hands and utilize formal titles and last names until you are asked to introduce them by their first names. Respect and courtesy are important to Slovaks in their dealings.

Dress modestly and refrain from wearing exposing apparel when visiting churches and other religious buildings. In the majority of other settings, casual clothing is typically appropriate.

Tipping: Although not required in Slovakia, good service is appreciated with a tip. In cafés and restaurants, it is traditional to tip 10%, while in taxis, it is typical to round up the total.

Slovakia has severe laws against smoking. Smoking is not allowed in enclosed public areas, such as bars, restaurants, and public transportation.

When shooting pictures of individuals, especially in formal or sacred contexts, always get their consent.

Communication and Language

Slovak is the official language of Slovakia. While younger generations and those who frequent tourist destinations speak English fluently, older citizens or those who live in some remote areas may not. It might be welcomed and useful to learn a few fundamental Slovak terms, such as courteous welcomes.

- *Hello: Ahoj (AH-hoy)*
- *Thank you: Ďakujem (JAH-koo-yem)*
- *Please: Prosím (PRO-seem)*
- *Yes: Áno (AH-no)*
- *No: Nie (Nee)*

- *Excuse me / Sorry: Prepáčte (pre-PAHCH-teh)*

If necessary, having a phrasebook or translation program on your phone will help you communicate with locals.

Your trip to Presov City will be more fun and hassle-free if you are prepared with useful information regarding emergency numbers, hospitals, local customs, and the language. Prior to your journey, always keep up with the most recent travel warnings and laws.

Tips and precautions for safety

Although it is typically safe to go to Presov City in Slovakia, it is important to use caution and be aware of any hazards. Here are some safety advice and measures to take into consideration while you are there:

Basic Safety Advice

Keep to crowded, well-lit locations, particularly at night. Avoid areas that are dark or empty since petty theft might happen there.

Be cautious of pickpockets and keep your possessions secure, especially in crowded tourist areas, marketplaces, and public transportation.

Avoid taking rides from strangers and instead use trusted, authorized taxis or ridesharing services.

Use ATMs with caution, and keep significant quantities of cash hidden from view. Use ATMs that are situated in secure, well-lit places.

Honor regional customs and laws. Learn about local laws, particularly those that *pertain to drinking and public conduct.*

A copy of your passport, identity, and information about your travel insurance should always be with you.

Use safety deposit boxes to store valuables and keep your place of residence securely closed.

Avoid having contentious conversations with locals regarding delicate political or cultural subjects as they can occasionally result in disagreements.

Awareness of Scams:

Travelers should be aware of possible scams and take care to avoid becoming victims of fraud even if Presov City is generally safe:

Be wary of people offering uninvited help, especially while exchanging money or booking lodgings.

To prevent getting overcharged, check pricing before making purchases or receiving services.

Be aware of con artists impersonating police officials or those who want money or aid while pretending to be in need.

Keep your credit card information and personal information private, particularly while utilizing public Wi-Fi networks.

To prevent frauds, do your research and reserve activities, excursions, and transportation from reliable and certified suppliers.

Awareness of Wildlife

Diverse fauna is part of Slovakia's natural attractiveness. Although coming into contact with animals might be exciting, it's important to follow safety precautions:

Avoid feeding wild animals since doing so might alter their behavior and cause potentially hazardous interactions.

Animals in the wild should not be approached or touched; instead, keep a safe distance from them.

Be cautious of potential wildlife interactions when hiking or exploring in nature reserves, such as wolves, lynx, and bears. Make noise to let animals know you are there and prevent them from being surprised.

When visiting protected regions and national parks, abide by the laws and regulations.

When trekking or camping in isolated regions, let someone know your plans and anticipated return time.

You may have a safe and pleasurable time while visiting Presov City by paying attention to these safety advice and measures, and you can appreciate Slovakia's natural beauty and rich cultural heritage without worrying. To guarantee an enjoyable and trouble-free trip, keep up with the most recent travel warnings and take the appropriate safety steps.

Responsible tourism and sustainable travel

You have the chance to have a positive influence on the area and the locals when you visit Presov City in Slovakia as a responsible tourist. Adopting sustainable travel habits and taking part in responsible tourism may assist in preserving the city's cultural legacy, safeguarding the environment, and assisting the neighborhood. A few tips for being a responsible traveler are as follows:

Respect for Local Traditions and Culture

Before going to Presov, learn about the local way of life. Understanding and honoring regional customs will improve your travel experience and demonstrate your respect for the host culture.

When visiting holy places and going to cultural events, dress modestly. This demonstrates respect for regional traditions and promotes local integration.

Be respectful and pleasant in your interactions with the populace. Slovak greetings and fundamental words may greatly enhance conversations.
Be aware of cultural nuances and abstain from actions that might be interpreted as

disrespectful or unsuitable in the local setting.

By purchasing genuine trinkets and handicrafts that pay homage to the area's cultural past, you can support regional artisans and craftspeople.

Ecologically sound practices

Reduce your environmental effect by using fewer resources and less trash. Reduce your consumption of single-use plastics by using reusable shopping bags and water bottles. Pick environmentally sustainable modes of transportation whenever feasible. Presov City may be explored on foot or by bicycle, which lowers carbon emissions while also letting you take in the culture of the area. Reduce your travel's carbon footprint by using public transportation or carpooling for longer trips. When leaving your accommodation, save energy by turning off the lights and the air conditioner.

Respect animals and natural environments. When touring nature reserves, keep to the established pathways and don't bother the wildlife.

Supporting Local Communities

Select lodgings, dining establishments, and tour companies that emphasize ethical and sustainable behavior. Search for eco-friendly lodgings that encourage recycling and energy efficiency.

Buy products and services made in your community and support local companies. This boosts the local economy and guarantees that the neighborhood immediately benefits from tourists.

Take part in community-based tourism activities to interact with locals and get knowledge about their culture.

Think about volunteering with recognized groups that benefit the neighborhood and environment. Always make sure that the needs and goals of the community are met by your volunteer activities.

Avoid buying anything created from rare, illicit, or endangered species of plants or plants that are endangered.

You may aid in the long-term preservation of Presov City's cultural legacy and natural beauty by adopting these sustainable travel and responsible tourism practices into your trip. By being a responsible visitor, you can ensure that present and future generations may take pleasure in and appreciate this alluring Slovakian location.

Concluding Remarks about Presov City

Every visitor to Slovakia's Presov City is left with a lasting impression because to its alluring combination of history, culture, and natural beauty. While the surrounding surroundings of the Carpathian Mountains and national parks offer a haven for nature lovers and outdoor enthusiasts, the historical center's well-preserved streets and architectural treasures transport you back in time.

A fuller knowledge of Presov's rich historical and multicultural past may be gained by touring its museums, galleries, and religious buildings. This picturesque location's attractiveness is heightened by the kind hospitality of the residents and their pride in their cultural heritage.

Presov's thriving nightlife, cultural activities, and festivals foster a dynamic environment and provide many possibilities to participate in regional customs and festivities.

In order to ensure that your visit positively contributes to the preservation and sustainability of Presov City, you should respect local culture, engage in ecologically beneficial practices, and give back to the community.

Slovakia, With Love

Bidding farewell to this stunning nation as your trip in Slovakia draws to a close is sad. The experiences you had at Presov City and elsewhere will live on in your heart forever. Slovakia surely made an impression on your travels, whether it was the High Tatras' breathtaking scenery or the kind residents.

Take with you a respect for the rich history and many cultures you have experienced as you leave Presov and Slovakia. Your journey has undoubtedly been enhanced by the friendliness and warmth of the folks you've encountered along the route.

May you take with you the spirit of responsible travel and the desire to see the world with an open mind and a courteous heart as you proceed to your next location.

Keep in mind the special encounters you had in Presov and value the relationships you formed there.

Slovakia, I'll miss you till our next encounter. Travelers will always be drawn by your allure and beauty to discover your mysteries and riches. May the memories of your stay in Slovakia bring you joy and thankfulness as you go on with your life's journey. Travel safely!

Appendix

Slovak phrases that are useful

- *Hello: Ahoj (AH-hoy)*
- *Good morning: Dobré ráno (DOH-breh RAH-noh)*
- *Good afternoon: Dobrý deň (DOH-bree dehn)*
- *Good evening: Dobrý večer (DOH-bree VEH-cher)*
- *Please: Prosím (PRO-seem)*
- *Thank you: Ďakujem (JAH-koo-yem)*
- *Yes: Áno (AH-no)*
- *No: Nie (Nee)*
- *Excuse me / Sorry: Prepáčte (pre-PAHCH-teh)*
- *Goodbye: Dovidenia (doh-vee-DYE-nyah)*
- *How much is this?: Koľko to stojí? (KOHL-koh toh STOH-yee?)*
- *Where is the restroom?: Kde je toaleta? (kdeh yeh TOH-ah-let-ah?)*

- *I don't understand: Nerozumiem (neh-roh-ZOO-myem)*
- *Help!: Pomoc! (POH-mots)*

Acknowledgments

For their warm welcome and eagerness to share their culture and customs with visitors, the people of Slovakia, especially those in Presov City, deserve our sincere appreciation. Many tourists' vacation experiences have been enhanced by their charity and friendliness.

We also like to express our gratitude to Presov's local government, companies, and organizations for their dedication to responsible tourism and sustainable travel. It is admirable that they are making an attempt to preserve the area's natural beauty and cultural legacy.

We would like to express our sincere thanks for helping you explore Presov City with the assistance of our guide.

We appreciate you picking the *Presov City Delight Travel Guide (2023)* to make your trip better. May you always treasure your experiences and be inspired by your trips.

Goodbye and safe travels!

Printed in Great Britain
by Amazon

39491417R00056